A

Baby

A

Gift

A Place to Collect

Your Precious Memories

A Baby – A Gift

Copyright © Angela Ashcraft
First Edition February 2019
Registration: #TXu 1-860-741 - April 25, 2013

Published in the United States of America
Philip L. Levin, production.
Doctor's Dreams Publishing
PO Box 4808
Biloxi, MS 39535

ALL RIGHTS RESERVED
No part of this book may be reproduced in any form without the written permission of the author, except for single pages to be used for promotion or commentary purposes.

ISBN: 978-1-942181-13-2

Dedication

*This book is dedicated to
James Robert Craven and
Johnathan Tyler Craven, my sons.*

For Stacey McCain for her help illustrating. She is legally blind in one eye.

My family for their support and love.

This Book belongs to:
Our precious little one that's true.

Things will be written about your start.
Words about how much you are loved
from our heart.

When we got the positive test
I felt such joy oh so blessed

The Things We Thought

DATE: TIME:

One little test can bring such joy! It doesn't matter if it's a girl or a boy.

You are a gift from God, that is true.
It's like a love I never knew.

God will guard and cherish you, little one
Until your days on this earth are done.

Your Baby Shower was full of laughter hour upon hour.

All wrapped up with tender loving care

Gifts and wrapping paper were everywhere

GUEST   GIFT

------------------   ------------------

------------------   ------------------

------------------   ------------------

------------------   ------------------

------------------   ------------------

------------------   ------------------

------------------   ------------------

------------------   ------------------

After all was said and done this shower was the most fun.

Clothes Pin Game

After food and the last game. I knew soon my life wouldn't be the same.

When I first heard your heart beat, I knew my life was complete

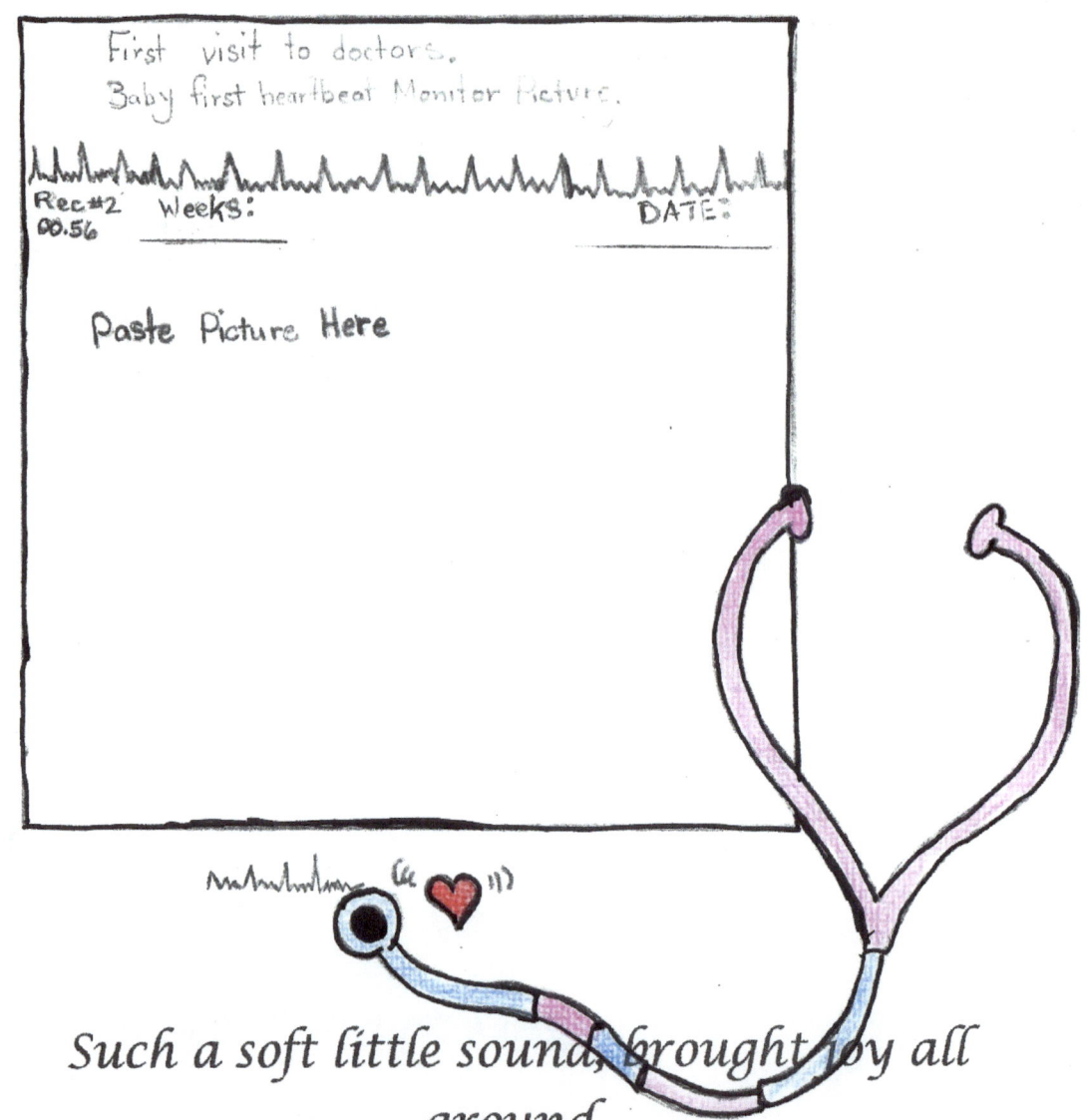

First visit to doctors.
Baby first heartbeat Monitor Picture.

Rec #2 00.56   Weeks: _____   DATE: _____

Paste Picture Here

Such a soft little sound, brought joy all around.

On the day you decided to arrive. To ---
--------------------hospital we took a drive.

Vroom! Vroom!

This little one

Needs more room!

As we sped on our way, we knew this was going to be a special night or day.

*Deep, deep inside mommy's womb,
You look so soft, so tiny, and so new.*

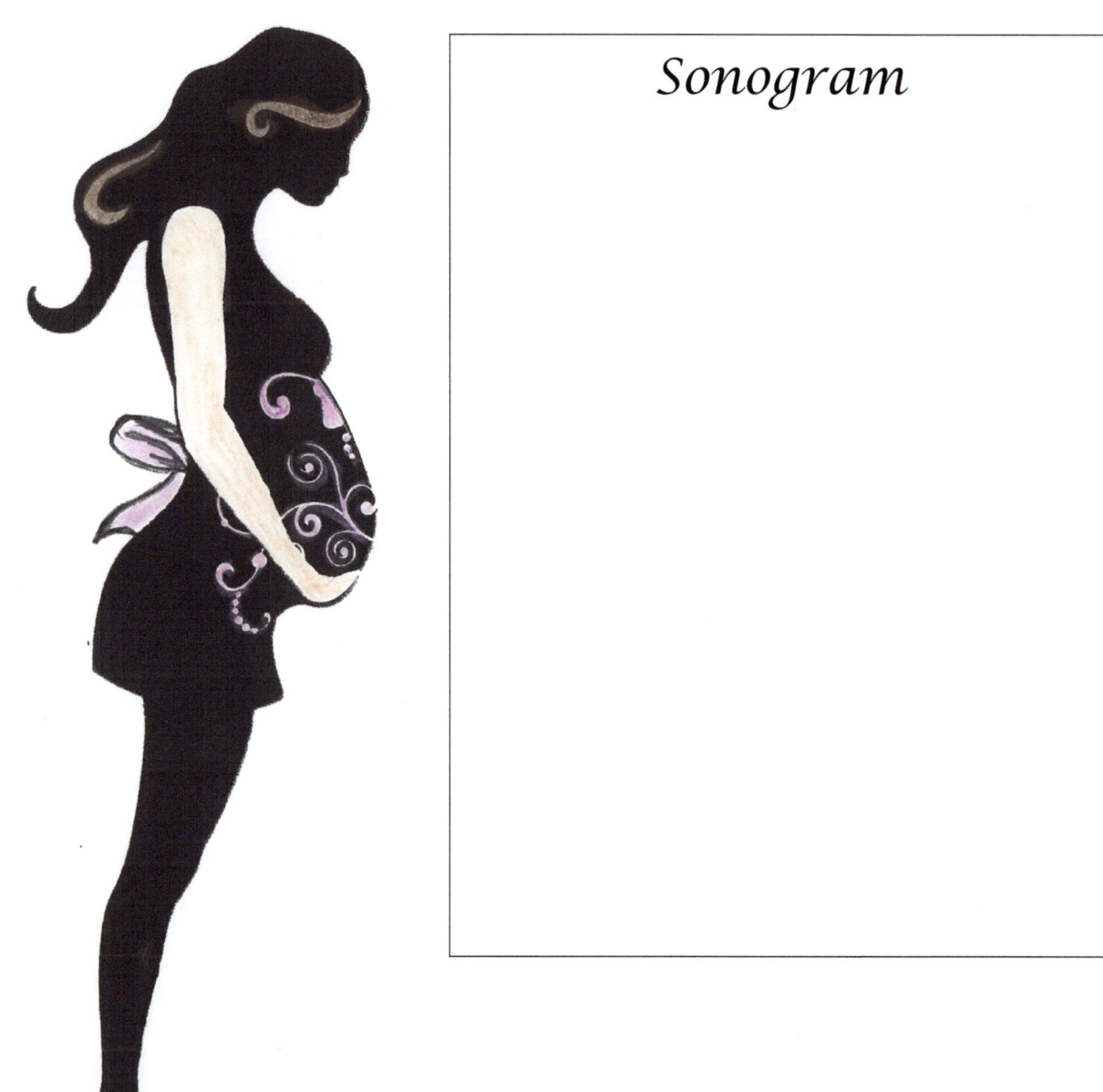

Sonogram

*It's real special having you grow inside of me.
God has blessed me and I'm so happy.*

The labor pains were coming fast!!! You were going to be here at last.

[Paste Picture Here]

As I breathed in and out, I wanted to slap, scream and shout

[Paste Picture Here]

Oh how we planned for this day! So much love and Joy more than words can say.

With the hurry and scurry of doctors and nurses all around you came out with a sweet crying sound

Paste Picture Here of new Baby

Oh how we prayed for you to make your day-view. The most precious gift that God has given is you.

You have a baby _____ the doctor said. Then he put you in my arms in my bed.

Picture of doctor placing baby in your arms

Your head was wrinkled and eyes opened wide.

At that moment I forgot the pain - only love was inside.

That was the most wonderful moment in time. I saw you when you just came out you were perfect and all mine.

Then they took you away to get us ready. I pray God will help me keep you on a path that is steady

The Nurses got you squeaky clean. As I watched it was like a wonderful dream.

With a cloth and a little tub,
Your first bath was a moment in time
I just loved.

The Nurses with care measured our precious little treasure.

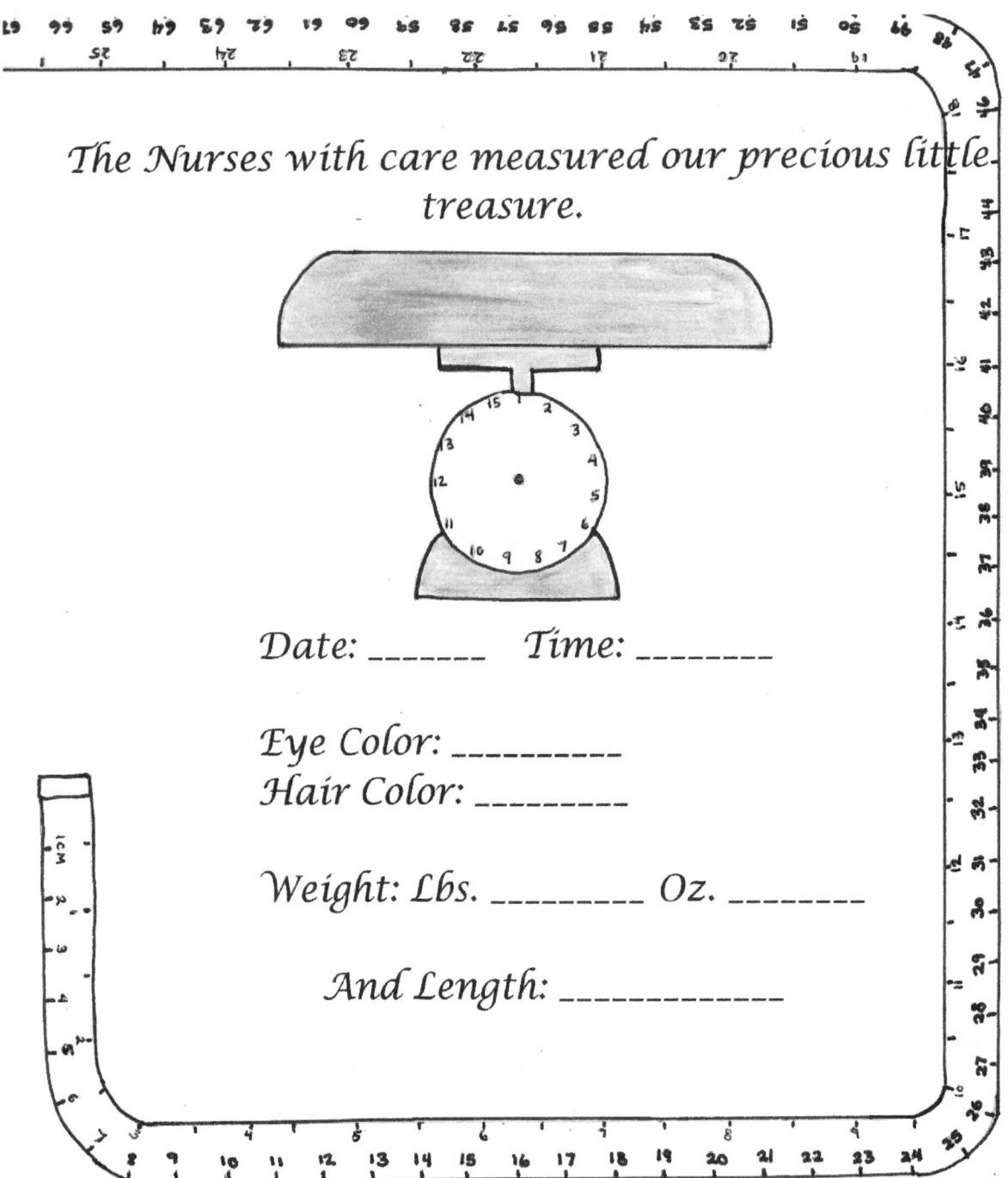

Date: _____ Time: _____

Eye Color: _____
Hair Color: _____

Weight: Lbs. _____ Oz. _____

And Length: _____

While you kicked & wiggled with all your strength.

A special name will be given_____
For this little life now out and living.

First: _____
Middle: _____
Last: _____

Some day you will make your mark on this earth. Just always remember how you were loved at your birth.

Here is how your birth we announced.
You're specially made with love, each and every ounce.

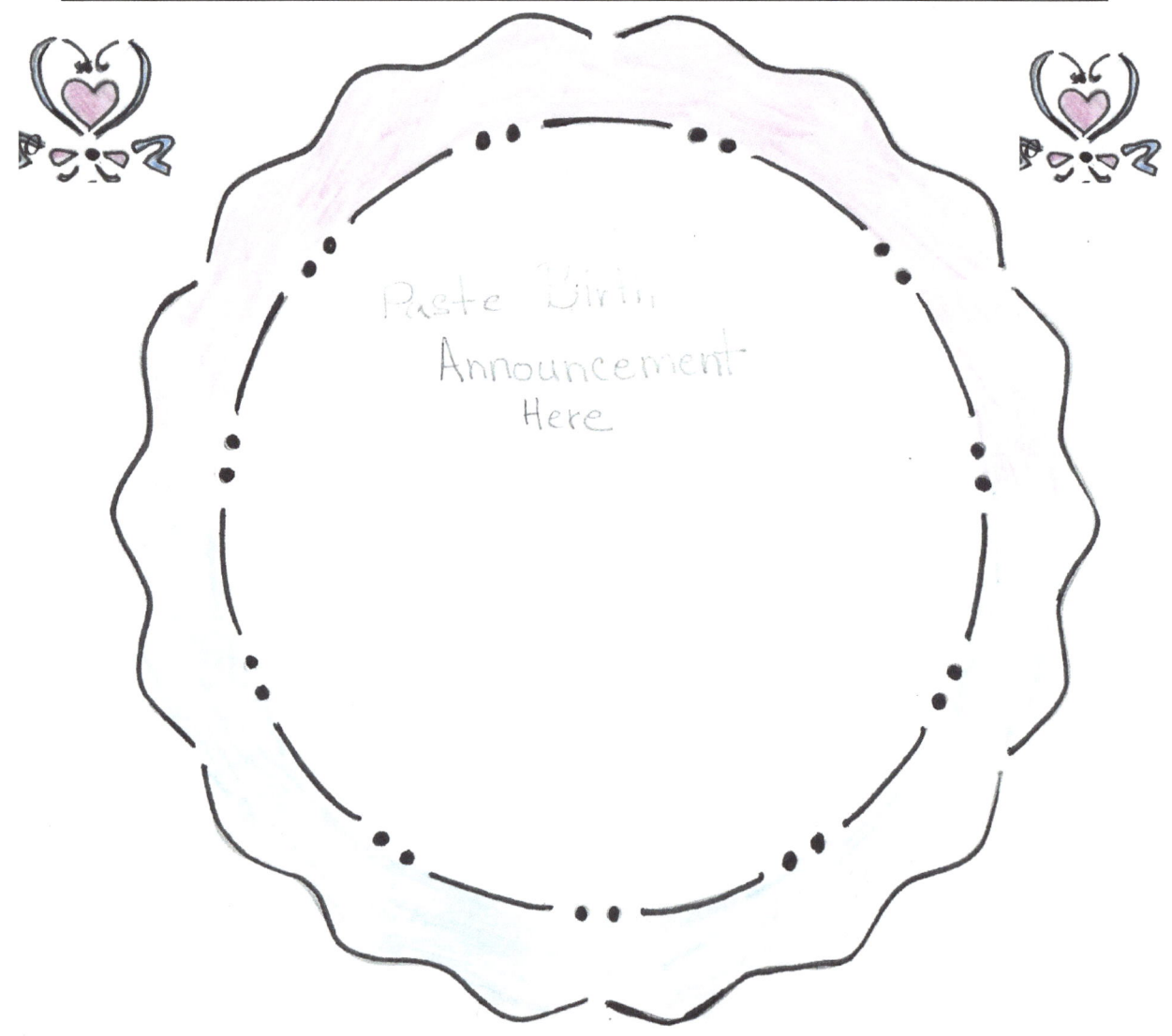

An ounce is small compared to you,
God's blessing from above,
So precious - so full of pure sweet love.

*This is your certificate of birth,
Because you were especially delivered to this earth.*

*God entrusted us in a wonderful way.
You're a joy to use each and every day.*

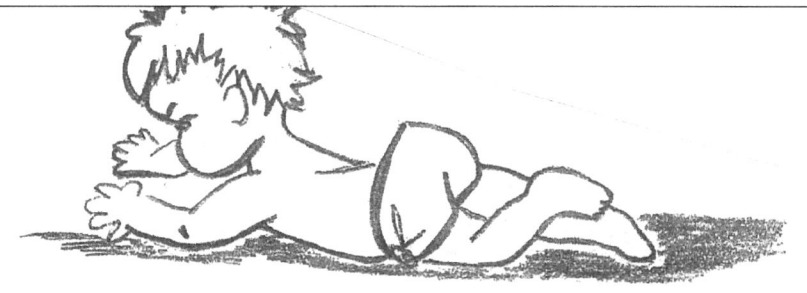

Your feeding time is always sweet.
Holding you is such a wonderful treat.

Each time you were hungry
I was there to feed your little tummy.

On your first stroller ride your eyes were open wide

With nature all around making a beautiful sound

There was a soft breeze as it blew through the leaves.

As I pushed you on a short walk just around the block

Your first smile:
Made my heart happy a long, long while.

I would love it when you would wiggle and giggle so I would tickle, tickle, tickle

The day you were given to our Lord is
a precious day we all adore.

The Celebration was a precious one.
With a blessing from God, Sprit and Son

You have sweet little hands and sweet little feet. Specially designed by God who made you unique.

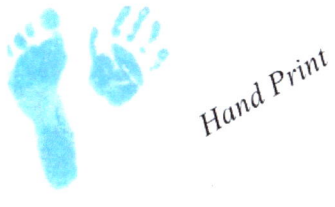 *Hand Print* 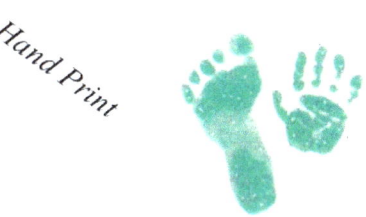 *Hand Print*

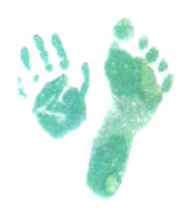 

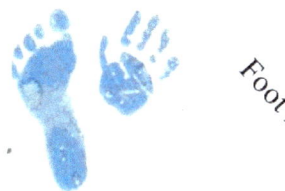 *Foot Print*  *Foot Print*

You are perfect with your little fingers and your toes. My love for you just grows and grows

When you rolled from front to back and back to front I recorded your first little stunt.

I had to get protective gear to protect your cute little rear.

When I heard your first sound,
I jumped and cheered all around.

GO_____

GO_____

You made your first sound
Kicked your feet and waved your hands around.

The first sound you made in my heart has stayed.
Pom-poms to cheer for the one I hold dear
This is the sound I did hear:

_____

Bath time is always lots of fun
When another day in your little life is done.

With a little scrub a dub-dub. You were washed in a little tub.

While you eat your first food, you
Puckered like I had done something
rude

You would taste it as I put it in you
push it out. So, so cute I laughed and
you would pout

When you scooted on your tummy for the first time. I knew busier days weren't far behind.

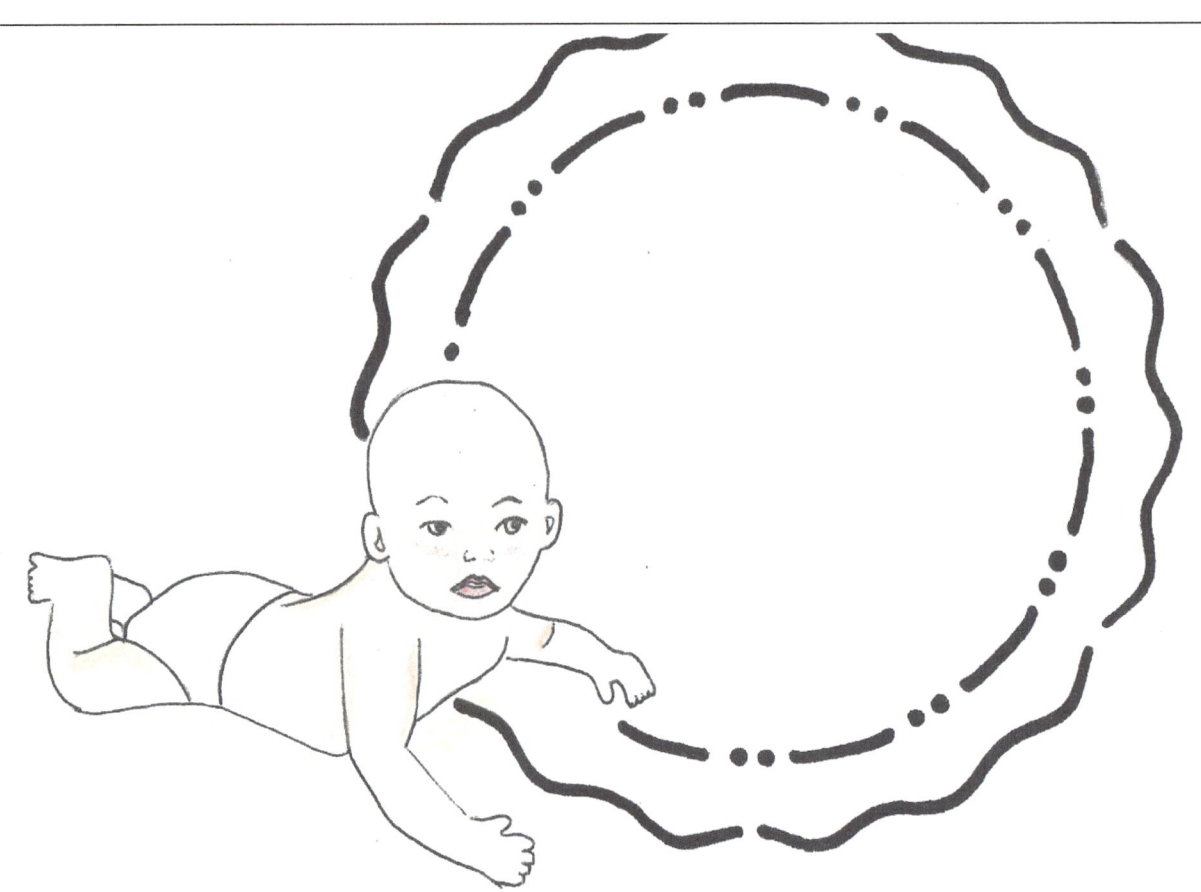

You would go up and down wiggle and squirm. Just like a cute little inch worm.

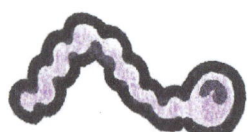 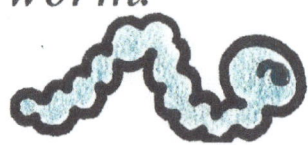 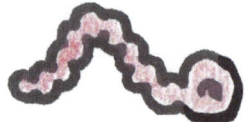

Now that you have learned to crawl on all four, you speed all over the floor.

I had so much fun you were like a bumper car. You were and still are my little bright star.

First Hair Cut

Just a lock of hair, saved from you with care.

Before   After

Put here for you to see,
how your hair looked when God first
made you to be.

When teething time came with a little fuss here and there I was there with lots of tender loving care.

I held you all night when you would cry,
And with a napkin I'd wipe your eye.

With a giggle and laugh here and there. Your' personality is coming out with flair.

Paste Picture Here

As God watches you with His eye, He giggles till He cries.

When I saw a tooth just poking through, I knew it was time for soft and cold things to chew.

God helped me with your all-night crying.
I prayed for patience, I'm not lying.

On this page I charted your doctor visits. Your shot and growth chart all listed

Age	Weight	Height	Shot
Birth			
Hospital Discharge			
One Month			
Two Month			
Three Month			
Four Month			
Five Month			
Six Month			
Seven Month			
Eight Month			
Nine Month			
Ten Month			
Eleven Month			
One Year			

So I could know for sure nothing was wrong. All the doctors were there to help you along.

After you took your first wobbly step
You started dancing with some pep.

Then you were into everything.
I just wanted to laugh and sing.

Bed time would come so fast, playing with you was such a blast.

We would do the bop, and then into bed you would drop.

The night you slept all through!!!! We weren't sure exactly what to do!!!

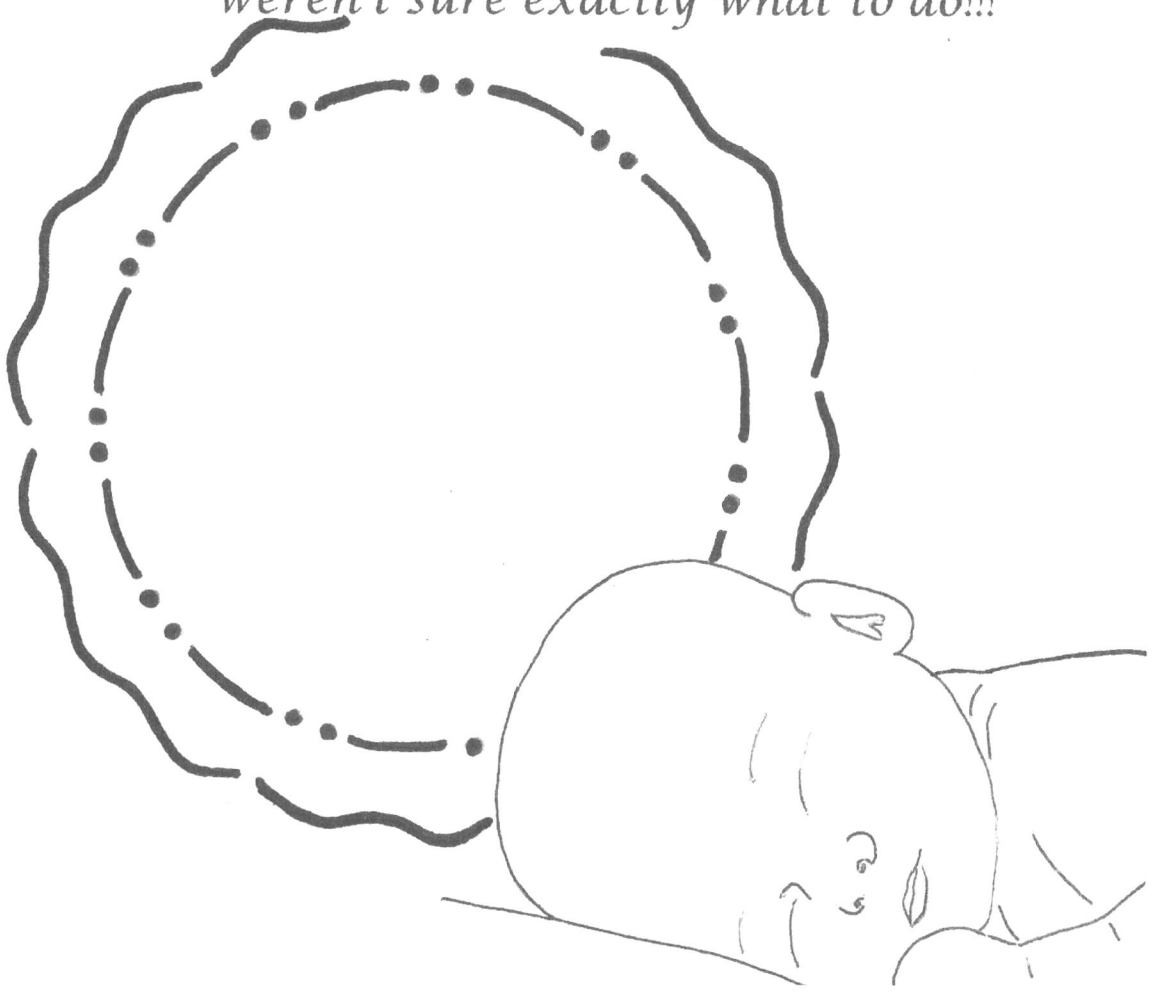

We kept peeking in your room – didn't sleep a wink. Splashing our faces at the bathroom sink.

EXTRA!!! EXTRA!!! News to be read and heard!!! Today you said your very first word!!!

It was such a shock!!! All these memories in my heart are locked.

AS I read to you every day, you learned new words to say.

Soon you out did me wow that I didn't foresee!!! HA HA

Here I recorded your family tree
So you'll know how you came to be.

Each family member is written on a
leaf to see. What a special tree.

I remember your first mark.
All over the walls your eyes light up like a spark.

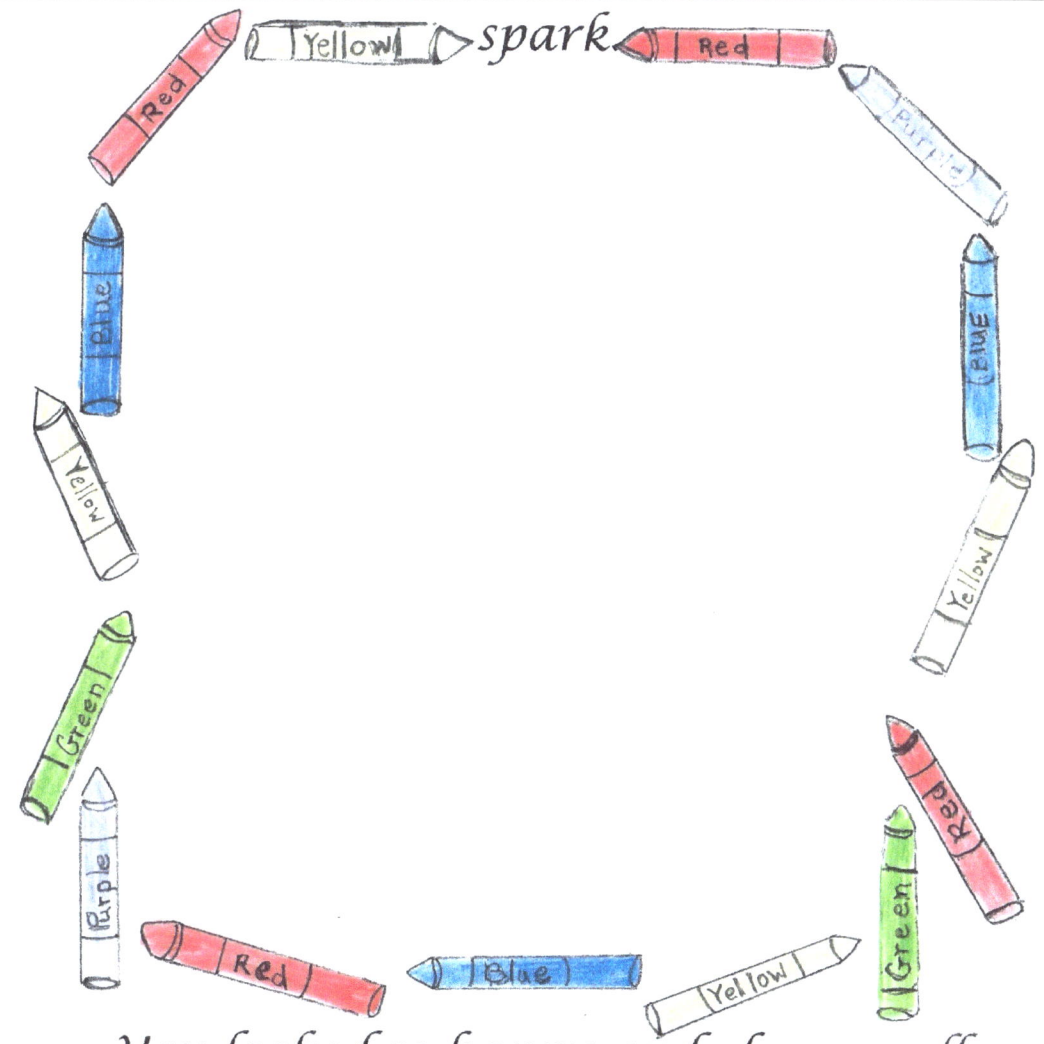

You looked so happy and oh so small.
We both scrubbed that wall!! HA HA

We celebrate the New Year watching
fireworks in the sky,
And tell your birth-year goodbye.

And say Hello to the year ahead. As
the day ends we slip into bed.

You had a happy fist Valentine
With cards and candy to make your heart shine.

You were so little yet had so much fun.
You passed out before the day was done.

You had a great first Saint Patricks' day, with stories of little green men and lots of play

Paste Picture Here

With people in green all around, we hunted for lucky four leaf clovers on the ground

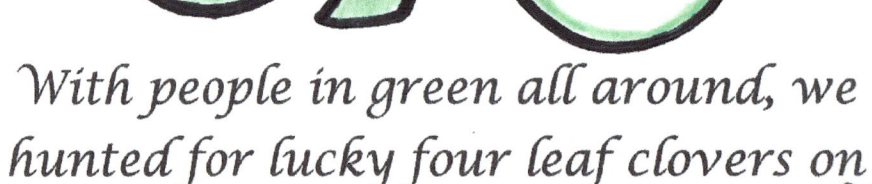

On your first Easter Holiday,
We bowed our hearts and heads to pray.

AS I held you in my arms, I prayed God
would keep you from all harms.

On your first Fourth of July
You watched with wonder in
your eyes

1ST

With fireworks lighting up the sky
Booms and flashes before your eyes.

ON Halloween we passed out candy.
And for light we had our jack-o-lanterns handy.

To light the way with little ghouls and goblins all around Making a fun giggling sound

Your first Thanksgiving was lots of fun,
With food and stories of what the

Indians and Pilgrims had done.

With decorations of turkeys, corn and squash we danced around. Using hands to our mouths to make a Indian sound.

Our most priceless holiday of all your first Christmas the birth of JESUS GOD'S SON.

GOD gave a priceless gift HIS SON. For all of us so we could be forgiven for all we have done

Your first birthday was a special time
Memories of this day will forever be
in our hearts and minds

AS you grow, grow, grow. You make
my heart glow, glow, glow.

You are a heaven sent GODS own blue print.

Specially made, specially designed from above. GODS gift from above.

This book was all about you, a gift from God above.
Filled with goodness and love.

The days sure have gone by fast.
Oh how I wish these days with you would forever last.

About the Author

Angela Ashcraft lives in Gautier, MS. She enjoyed her two sons' first year and had such fun with them, she decided to share her dream of memorializing their infancy with photos by creating this photo and poetry book.

She hopes that with this book you will be able to make sweet memories of your precious little one.

Angela suffers from bipolar disorder and finds that her writing helps her stay focused and positive.

www.ingramcontent.com/pod-product-compliance
Lightning Source LLC
Chambersburg PA
CBHW060757090426
42736CB00002B/64